To _____,
a great Sunday school teacher

with gratitude from _____

Date _____

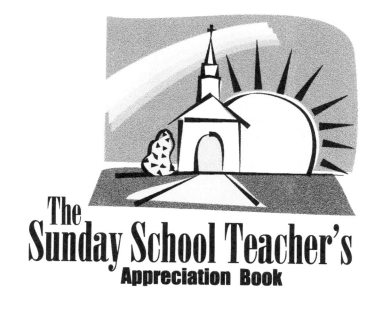

The Sunday School Teacher's
Appreciation Book

Compiled by Linda Washington

Harold Shaw Publishers
Wheaton, Illinois

© 1998 Harold Shaw Publishers

Every effort has been made to contact copyright holders for materials that do not fall into the public domain or fair use categories. If any acknowledgment was inadvertently omitted, the publisher expresses regret.

Cover and inside design by David LaPlaca
Edited by Elizabeth Cody Newenhuyse

ISBN 087788-793-4

Library of Congress Cataloging-in-Publication Data

The Sunday school teacher's appreciation book / compiled by Linda Washington.
     p.   cm.
   ISBN 0-87788-793-4 (pbk.)
   1. Sunday school teachers—Quotations. 2. Sunday school teachers—Anecdotes. I. Washington, Linda M.
BV1534.S84 1998
268'.3—dc21
                                       98-46776
                                       CIP

---

03 02 01 00 99 98
10 9 8 7 6 5 4 3 2 1

Acknowledgments

"A Solution for Crime?" by Chuck Colson is taken from *Teacher Touch*, Summer 1997, and is reprinted with permission of Prison Fellowship, P. O. Box 17500, Washington, D.C. 20041-0500.

All Scripture quotations, unless otherwise indicated, are taken from the HOLY BIBLE, NEW INTERNATIONAL VERSION ®. NIV ® Copyright © 1973, 1978, 1984 International Bible Society. Used by permission of Zondervan Publishing House. All rights reserved.

The "NIV" and "New International Version" trademarks are registered in the United States Patent and Trademark Office by International Bible Society. Use of either trademark requires permission of International Bible Society.

Scripture quotations marked NLT are taken from the *Holy Bible*, New Living Translation, copyright © 1996. Used by permission of Tyndale House Publishers, Inc., Wheaton, Illinois 60189. All rights reserved.

Scripture quotations marked TLB are taken from *The Living Bible*, copyright © 1971. Used by permission of Tyndale House Publishers, Inc., Wheaton, Illinois 60189. All rights reserved.

What's Inside

Now you are the body of Christ, and each one of you is a part of it. And in the church God has appointed first of all apostles, second prophets, third teachers.

1 Corinthians 12:27-28

Introduction

Thanks for Being on the Team!

How is a Sunday school teacher like a baseball player?

Ballplayers and other sports figures know the value of being part of a team, especially a team that works well together and wins championships! You're part of a winning team, too—a team of Sunday school teachers helping to spread the gospel. As 1 Corinthians 3:8-9 (NLT) says, "The one who plants and the one who waters work as a team with the same purpose. Yet they will be rewarded individually, according to their own hard work. We work together as partners who belong to God."

There are many people out there, just like you—people from all walks of life who value the teaching of God's Word. Members of the team include corporation executives, former presidents of the United States, and well-known ministry leaders.

I too am part of this special team. I come from a family of Sunday school teachers. Both of my parents are lifelong teachers. My brother Stan and my sister-in-law, Gia, are also Sunday school teachers. You'll hear from some of them in this book.

This book is for anyone who teaches Sunday school or who wants to say a hearty "thank you" to those who teach Sunday school. As Ray Boltz mentioned in his song "Thank You," "I am a life that was changed" as a result of a Sunday school teacher's influence. As a teacher, you may not always be aware of the impact you have on the kids and adults you minister to on a weekly basis. That's why some of your "teammates," Sunday school teachers from around the country, have gathered to remind you of the impact you have and to share their experiences and enthusiasm for Sunday school. So get ready. There's a box seat with your name on it.

Linda Washington

Hall-of-Famers

Teachers Remembered

Dear brothers and sisters, honor those who are your leaders in the Lord's work. They work hard among you and warn you against all that is wrong. Think highly of them and give them your wholehearted love because of their work.

1 Thessalonians 5:12-13 (NLT)

Teachers are gifts God gave the body of Christ. But Sunday school teachers are among the unsung heroes of the world. Some grateful students pause to say thanks for the life-changing lessons they learned.

The Woman Who Lived the Story

My first contact with living story was Miss Bennett. I was in my early teens, a product of Sunday-after-Sunday school. I knew all the stories and even practiced telling them to the preschool class. I don't remember when the words *flannelgraph* and *flash cards* were not part of my vocabulary. But Miss Bennett didn't just tell stories; she became stories. She was ancient and wrinkled, with her slip hanging out, a funny little hat and veil on top of her head. I knew the minute I saw her the first time that there was no way I was going to listen to her—and then she began to talk. Without any aids, she talked me up the long road to Calvary and made me participate in the pain and dust and flies and smells of that awful Jerusalem day. This adolescent, sophisticated Sunday school snob was captured by the reality of a story.

Marlene LeFever
Editor, Teacher Touch

Lifelong Security

My preschool Sunday school teacher let God love me through her and I have had a security in his love throughout my life as a result.

Elsie Lippy
Editor, Evangelizing Today's Child

Loving the Word

My fifth-grade Sunday school teacher used to bring and read from *The Living Bible*, which had just been published. When she read from the Bible, I could tell she loved it and believed God was speaking to her. I had never seen a person read it in that way before—my parents were not Christians—and I was moved by it. She made me want to get closer to God.

Kevin A. Miller
Vice-president, Christianity Today, Inc.

From One Teacher to Another

When I think of Sunday school, I naturally think of Mrs. Hazel Farley. She taught our junior class with an enthusiasm and warmth that launched me where I am today, as an editor and a writer of Sunday school curriculum. I can still see her as she was so many years ago, repositioning those flannelgraph pieces that always fell off the board; gently reining in the giggles and wisecracks that always bubbled out of ten and eleven year olds. Years later, in that same Baptist church, I had my own class of giggling ten and eleven year olds. Talk about passing the torch. Thanks, Mrs. Farley!

Linda Washington

Dear friend, you are faithful in what you are doing.

3 John 5

Because Phoebe Cared

I was a shy little girl. I didn't get to Sunday school very often. One of my favorite visitors was Phoebe Anderson. She came to the farm from time to time to see how I was doing and to chat with my parents. Phoebe, who taught second grade in the public schools, knew how to be a friend to kids and to their families. She liked to talk to me because I was important to her, and so was everything I had to say.

At Sunday school, I could always count on Phoebe (she *was* Phoebe, *not* Miss Anderson) being there. She was my teacher, and she was the primary superintendent for many years. I don't remember any specific stories or lessons. But I do remember that going to Sunday school meant seeing Phoebe, who cared about me and wanted me to be there. When I grew up and became an editor of Sunday school curriculum, I thought about Phoebe. And I knew that as important as the lessons were that I helped to develop, they weren't nearly as important as the Phoebe Andersons and the love that they share each week with the young children in their classes.

Betty Free
Children's Book Editor, Tyndale House Publishers

Ornaments and More

When I was in third grade, my Sunday school teacher invited our class to her home. We painted ceramic Christmas ornaments together. I still have mine. She told us about a time when God answered a prayer in her life. I felt like she cared about me and I was inspired by her story. I knew she took God and her Sunday school material seriously. She really believed.

Margie Clark
Director of Children's Ministries
Church of the Resurrection, Wheaton, Illinois

An Anointing to Teach

My most memorable Sunday school teacher was Deacon Eddie Phillips. He was a man with very limited formal education and was far from eloquent in his delivery. Yet, his knowledge of the Scriptures and the passion with which he taught could literally mesmerize you. Without a doubt, if anyone had both a calling and an anointing to teach, he most certainly would get my vote.

Edward E. Hearn
Pastor, Grace Conservative Baptist Church, Chicago

"I'll Never Forget"

Moments That Meant Something

Well done, good and faithful servant! You have been faithful with a few things; I will put you in charge of many things. . . . Come and share your master's happiness.

Matthew 25:21-23

Some teachers will tell you that there were moments that made them realize how glad they were God called them to teach. Their students might recall moments when Sunday school had a special meaning for them. Here are some of those moments.

Lighthouse in L.A.

My fondest memory of Sunday school is framed by the sun-drenched stuccoed sprawl of Los Angeles in the early fifties, through which my family trekked from the suburbs to the lovely Scottish Kirk ambience of Vermont Avenue Presbyterian Church. There we were ushered to our seats by a man dressed in blue serge with a white carnation in his lapel. After listening to a reverent exposition by the Geneva-gowned pastor, we children exited down a dark hallway lined by cases filled with missionary artifacts to Sunday school. The apex of my third grade Sunday experience was singing "Heavenly Sunshine" as we placed our offerings in an enameled steel lighthouse and watched the light flash with each coin. The scene still graces my life. The church is to be a life-saving station signaling hope and a safe harbor—salvation in a dark world.

R. Kent Hughes
Pastor, College Church, Wheaton, Illinois

More Than Words

A young man who was my student in third grade Sunday school keeps in touch with me. He is currently a high school senior. Over the years, he has called me at least monthly to share his life's story and events. It says that I changed his life by loving him and showing him that the Bible was more than words.

On another occasion, a family joined the church because the young child so wanted to come to Sunday school that she encouraged her parents to attend. Later they joined the church and found Christ.

Walter Shiffer
Speaker and seminar leader with the Chicago Sunday School Association

This I Know

I began Sunday school when I was four. . . . Our teachers told us stories about the Bible, or helped us make religious posters, or led us in singing.

Jesus loves me! this I know,
For the Bible tells me so;
Little ones to him belong;
They are weak, but He is strong.

Later as we grew older there would be more sophisticated Sunday school sessions when we would sit in small circles and talk about religion and how we could get the children who had not showed up that Sunday more interested in it. We would hold hands and pray, and whisper the benediction, and dream up projects to make our class the most active in the whole church and how best to help out the preacher in his many duties. We would read Bible verses and discuss their hidden meaning.

Willie Morris
Former editor-in-chief of Harper's *magazine*

Little Learning, Much Zeal

My fondest memories of Sunday school include the time of my youth when the teacher could barely read but had the zeal necessary to create a desire in the young children to attend each Sunday. He had the foresight to make us read and explain verses in the simple Sunday school book. We also had to explain the picture roll [a flip chart type of lesson that was hung on an easel and had a picture and a Scripture that followed the lessons] and the blackboard. [A statement from the day's lesson was copied onto the blackboard to be explained by a student or teacher to the assembly.] Each kid was proud to be called on to stand in front of the assembly that always followed the lesson to tell what he/she learned in class. I treasured those times and went on to teach all different grades.

Preston Washington,
A Sunday school teacher and full-time public school teacher

Love in a Special Package

One Sunday morning, as the new pastor of the church, I walked through the children's department at opening time. The teacher for one class of boys eight to ten years old was late. The boys were like you would expect guys that age to be: talking loudly, moving around the room, laughing—just short of a friendly wrestling match. Five minutes later, a man in his forties burst through the door, breathing hard from running. His hair was bushy, and he gestured wildly as he said, "All right, you guys, sit down and shut up." Instantly the boys sat down and looked admiringly at their teacher. It was obvious that the teacher and students knew and understood each other. The lesson was taught in a gruff voice with pointed language, and the teacher closed with a simple prayer. The boys were mesmerized.

Dr. T. O. Thomas
Pastor of the seniors ministry
Sugar Creek Baptist Church, Texas

The Tough Questions

I was always a little surprised when kids would ask difficult questions, like how would someone get AIDS and if there really was a Santa Claus. Obviously, they felt that they could ask these questions and get an honest answer from me. That is the biggest compliment I could receive as a Sunday school teacher.

Pat Bradley
Director of Adoptions, Lifelink, Bensenville, Illinois

A President's Faith

Religious faith has always been at the core of my existence. It has been a changing and evolving experience, beginning when I was a child of three, memorizing Bible verses in Sunday school. When I was nine years old, I was promoted to the Sunday school class taught by my father, so I had the double influence of the church environment and my own father as a teacher. My faith at first was simple and unequivocal; there was no doubt in my mind about the truth of what I learned in church.

Jimmy Carter

Self-Expression

My fondest memory of Sunday school is being able to express myself without being judged critically by others in the class. It influenced me this way: I teach the high school students in my church and I encourage them often to express themselves too without judging them.

Yvonne Hearn

He Taught by Who He Was

When I think of my Sunday school experience, I think of children's church and, especially, Mr. Courrier, the pastor who led the mini-service. It was held in a venerable chapel with whitewashed stucco walls, stained-glass windows, and old yellow light fixtures hanging from a high, beamed ceiling. The place almost *smelled* holy; it had that solemn, dress-in-your-best feeling you don't get in today's contemporary buildings. On sunny mornings it appeared to be suffused with golden light. I recall being very bored by the classroom part of the Sunday school hour, but I loved the feeling of sitting in the old wooden pews, learning hymns, praying, and—especially—listening to Mr. Courrier.

I thought he was a saint. He was young, with a pale, reverent brow, curly hair, and a gentle manner. By eighth grade I had a full-blown crush on him, but it was a chaste, worshipful sort of admiration. He was just so . . . *good*. He made me want to be in church. I couldn't put it into words at the time, but I now realize that he taught by who he was. His example pointed me toward Christ. Not right then and there; there were to be a few more twists and turns before I finally yielded to the Lord, but something of his spirit spoke to my spirit, saying, in effect, "There's a narrow and shining road out there. Someday you will discover it, or it will discover you—and, perhaps, when you tread it you might think of me."

Tragically, Mr. Courrier died young, in an accident, and one wonders how many more souls he could have touched for the kingdom. But here's a soul who's eternally grateful.

Elizabeth Cody Newenhuyse

Train up a child in the way he should go, and walk there yourself once in a while.

Josh Billings

The Difference It Makes

Why We Need Sunday School

These commandments that I give you today are to be upon your hearts. Impress them on your children.

Deuteronomy 6:6-7

A famous 1957 article in Life *magazine declared that Sunday school was sometimes "the most wasted hour of the week." But there are many who would disagree with that statement. If you're wondering about what impact Sunday school has on a kid (or an adult), keep reading.*

Experiencing God with Others

When I was a little girl, Sunday school represented a time to occasionally learn something while enjoying the company of friends. As I grew older, it took on the opposite effect. I began to appreciate the learning experience in an environment I felt comfortable in.

I think this is extremely important for both children and adults. No matter what stage of life we're in, we need to experience God with others who are in a similar stage. This provides us with encouragement, support, thought provocation, and accountability, among other things.

We may not remember everything we're taught in Sunday school, but the experience itself helps us to grow in our Christian walk. It has advantages that can't be absorbed by sitting idle in a packed congregation.

Whether we're six years old or sixty, Sunday school can enrich our lives in a powerful way. It has for me!

Danae Dobson

Full Circle

I chose my career because I was influenced by two Sunday school teachers. My junior high teacher was totally blind. He taught me how to do audio recordings. Together we wrote and recorded Christian "radio programs" for class. In high school I had a young teacher who got me interested in video. My work was used in class, club, and the main worship service. Today I'm vice president of a video company, and frequently use my skills to produce videos to teach Sunday school teachers. How's that for God's full circle!

Darren Gould, as quoted by Marlene LeFever in Learning Styles

A cheerful look brings joy to the heart, and good news gives health to the bones.

Proverbs 15:30

Tough but Rewarding

Sunday school was a part of my life since my early childhood. As a girl in Centerville, Tennessee, I listened to many a Sunday school lesson and came under the influence of a variety of teachers. . . . During my young adult years, I too was a Sunday school teacher, so I can identify with all of you who are now teaching a class. You deserve lots of stars in your crown. Teaching Sunday school is a tough but rewarding task. It can also be lots of fun, and it definitely can be the source of many laughs.

Minnie Pearl, quoted in The Official Sunday School Teachers Handbook

Moral Impact

Sunday school sets the foundation for a child's spiritual learning. Children are taught at their own level of learning by an impartial adult, not by parents whom they may not listen to. Children's sense of trust is enhanced when they are taught by a teacher they respect who can share the truth with them. I think Sunday school can impact a child's moral and character development as [he or she] learns from the Bible how to treat others and right from wrong.

Pat Bradley

Fun Stuff That Isn't Boring

[Our Sunday school teacher] is a cool teacher who always wants to know what we think about stuff. Then she always helps us think about what Jesus would do. And we do it by doing fun stuff that isn't boring and we usually end up learning something.

A statement jointly written by a fourth-sixth grade class

Who Kids Would Invite to Sunday School

In the Spring 1998 issue of Teacher Touch, *students were asked whom they would like to invite to Sunday school. Here are some of their suggestions:*

- "President Clinton. The United States would be in a lot better shape if all our leaders went to Sunday school" (Ben, 14).

- "Hudson Taylor. It would be neat to hear stories from a missionary from China, especially someone so famous" (Laura, 12).

- "Dr. Kevorkian. He's helped a lot of people commit suicide. He's a good talker. Think what a good preacher he'd make if he taught the Word instead of what he's doing now" (Brent, 11).

- "Hitler. He really had a messed-up head, and learning about God in Sunday school could have fixed that" (Asher and Clynt, both 13).

- "[My] cousin Samuel. He fights a lot with his brother, and in Sunday school he'd learn not to do that" (Jade, 9).

- "Jesus. He could teach our class, and my teacher would get a break" (Adryan, 10).

- "Dennis Rodman. I think he really, really needs to learn about Jesus" (Marie, 11).

Rachael's Thanks

Last week was Youth Sunday at our church. Rachael Bergman was confirmed at this special service. About ten years ago, Rachael was a student in my preschool class. We had many good times together, singing, doing action rhymes, playing games, acting out stories, and making simple items to take home. I was an editor of Sunday school curriculum at the time, so it was always enlightening to see what worked and what didn't.

For her confirmation, Rachael looked so grown up in her white robe. Our pastor asked her to share some of her spiritual journey with the congregation. He asked her to tell about some of the people who had influenced her when she was young. Tears came to my eyes as I heard Rachael say, "Betty Free was my first Sunday school teacher, and she showed me that learning about Jesus can be fun." Such a simple statement, but how much it meant to me. God was allowing me to hear that I had been responsible for at least one little girl's enthusiasm for learning about Jesus.

Betty Free

A Solution for Crime?

When I was at Buckingham Palace . . . Prince Philip asked me, "What can we do about crime here in England?" I replied, "Send more children to Sunday school." He thought I was joking. But I pointed out a study by sociologist Christie Davies, which found that in the first half of the 1800s, British society was marked by high levels of crime and violence, which dropped dramatically in the late 1800s and early 1900s. What changed an entire nation's national character? Throughout that period, attendance at Sunday schools rose steadily until, by 1888, a full 75 percent of children in England were enrolled.

Since then, attendance has fallen off to one-third its peak level, with a corresponding increase in crime and disorder. If we fill the Sunday schools, we can change hearts and restore society.

Chuck Colson, quoted in Teacher Touch

When Christ Became Real

Joseph Bayly . . . [told] a story of a woman who had gone through her Sunday school years without having it touch her much at all. No doubt her teachers felt they had failed in their work with her. But as a young adult she suddenly faced an experience that she couldn't handle by herself. "I came to the end of my rope," she said. "Suddenly I remembered some of the things my Sunday school teachers had shared with me all those many years ago, and Christ became real to me. How I wish I could find those old teachers and give them a big thank-you hug."

Marlene LeFever

Absolutely Necessary

No matter what views are taken on general education, we all agree—Protestant, Catholic, and Jew alike—that Sunday-school education is absolutely necessary to secure moral uplift and religious spirit.

William Howard Taft

Why It Matters

Sunday school is important in the lives of children and adults because it serves as the initial exposure to the Bible and its teachings. It serves as the foundation for the building of Christian knowledge and its application to life. Sunday school provides opportunities for urban and suburban kids to develop a stronger sense of decision-making power as it relates to making appropriate life choices. In addition, Sunday school allows them to have a forum for clarifying issues that are a part of their lives. They can use the time in class to discuss areas of concern and to receive instruction on appropriate action to address those concerns.

James Meeks
Senior pastor, Salem Baptist Church, Chicago,
a church with one of the largest Sunday schools in the city

Little Parts of the Body

A highlight of our church's worship service is the weekly appearance of Belmont T. Bear. Belmont is a large, brown hand puppet, with a permanently bewildered expression, used by our children's ministries director, Mimi Larson, in her "word to the children" segment of the service. These messages teach the kids *and* the adults. They also have the effect of making younger children feel part of the worshiping community and helping adults to see them in that community.

On the Sunday our church was installing a new pastor, Mimi used the occasion to teach Belmont and the children about the importance of supporting and praying for the pastor. In a memorable and touching moment, good sport Pastor Rick sat cross-legged on the floor of the sanctuary while the children circled him and Mimi said a prayer for his ministry. It was a vivid illustration that even those in the toddler class are an integral part of the body of Christ.

Elizabeth Cody Newenhuyse

An Eternal Difference

Sunday school is still the most effective avenue for communicating the truths of God's Word. Sunday school can have a life-changing impact on children who connect with teachers who model godliness. Your efforts can make an eternal difference in young lives, even though you may not see that difference now.

Pat Conner, Director of Children's Ministries
Sugar Creek Baptist Church
Sugar Land, Texas

Seven Purposes of Religious Education

1. To lead the pupil into a personal relationship with God.

2. To give the pupil an understanding and appreciation of the life and teachings of Jesus, to lead him or her to accept Christ as Savior, Friend, Companion, and Lord, and to lead him or her into loyalty to Christ and his cause.

3. To lead to a progressive development of Christian character.

4. To lead into enthusiastic and intelligent participation of the building of a Christian community and world.

5. To develop the ability and desire to participate in the life and work of the church.

6. To give a Christian interpretation of life and the universe.

7. To give a knowledge, an understanding, and a love of the Bible.

Cyclopedia of Bible Illustrations

In the Beginning

How Teachers Got Started

A wise teacher makes learning a joy.

Proverbs 15:2 (TLB)

Every teacher has a story to tell about how he or she began teaching or why he or she continues to do so. Here are some of the stories of great starts and encouragement that led to lifelong memories.

Miracle Stories

Each teacher has a story, and from a spiritual perspective each story is a miracle, an affirmation that God is involved in our teaching.

Marlene LeFever

Godsend at the Doorstep

My introduction to teaching children came when I agreed to teach Bible school. I had been asked to find someone to teach with me. That seemed to be my most difficult assignment, as almost everyone I knew was already committed.

While standing at the kitchen sink washing up the lunch dishes, I prayed, "Lord, if you want me to teach send me someone to help me." Almost immediately the doorbell rang. There stood an attractive young woman selling

World Book encyclopedias. After some conversation we realized that we attended the same church. "Would you consider helping me teach?" Yes, she said, she would.

Now, thirty-five years later with only a few years when we were unable to do so, we continue to teach together. Thank you, God for answered prayer!

Jane Cory
Veteran teacher

Using the Gift

Sunday school is the place where I learned that the "giants" the minister preached about in the days of David are still very much alive and well today!

Sunday school laid the foundation for my early awareness of the Word of God. When I was a child, my parents literally made me go to Sunday school! And I always thought to myself, *As soon as I grow up, I'm outta here!* Nevertheless, as God worked in my life, I came to see that Sunday school was very foundational to my knowledge of biblical truth. So I've always loved being in Sunday school, as a result. I teach our new members class at church. However, even if I wasn't a pastor, I'd teach Sunday school, because it allows you to "connect" with people who really want more out of their walk with the Lord. So, since I'm aware that teaching is one of my spiritual gifts, I would be dishonoring God if I didn't use the gift he has given, and share in the joy it brings to those who attend.

Edward E. Hearn

God's Tool

I love Sunday school and have dedicated my life in its ministry. I still believe Sunday school is the most powerful tool that God has in his hand. I faithfully attend a class, and teach every opportunity I get. The Sunday school is the church at work . . . reaching . . . teaching . . . winning the lost . . . then training them for Christian service.

Elmer Towns
Author, The Successful Sunday School and Teachers Guidebook

Growth in Grace

For many years, my wife, Rose, and I worked with young married couples. Several of those we taught are now deacons, teachers, and ministers in a church. They have told me on many occasions that what they learned in my classes has been the foundation on which they have continued to study the Word of God, and to grow in grace and knowledge of the Lord.

Mike Harrison
Teacher of an adult Sunday school class, Sugar Creek Baptist Church

Carter's Commitment

After I left the navy and returned home to Plains, Georgia, I taught young boys and girls in Sunday school regularly for about fifteen years, as my father had always done when I was a child. Even as President, while I was attending Washington's First Baptist Church, the regular teacher and I would set aside a few Sundays each year for me to teach the adult class.

Jimmy Carter

Driven to Teach

I teach Sunday school because it is something that I love to do. I am actually driven to teach Sunday school. Although at times I do not feel like teaching or that I am worthy or prepared to teach, I still enjoy the lesson and the results when the class is over. I believe that God has given me the ability to guide some people through the Scriptures.

Stan Washington

"Why Not?"

I've taught Sunday school to kids, but early on—probably about the time I was playing "Bible Hangman" with my second-grade charges instead of following the regular lesson—I discovered it wasn't my gift, which is why I greatly admire those who do teach children year in, year out.

What I get really excited about is teaching adults. You don't have to be good at crafts, for one thing; and I have a passion for helping others grow in the Lord. I love leading discussions that relate God's Word to everyday life, which often means asking the right questions, drawing out that quiet person who may need a bit of encouragement.

How I got started: A few years back my husband and I decided to co-lead a Sunday-morning group. Teachers were needed, so our response was a "Why not?" Jump in first, figure out what you're doing later. We recruited a few people we knew to be mature believers who would speak up in discussions, but then the Holy Spirit took care of the rest, bringing a healthy mix of longtime members, newcomers, younger and older people. More than my teaching from the top down, we all learned from each other. So as long as I can keep learning, I'll keep teaching.

Elizabeth Cody Newenhuyse

Golden Apples for the Teacher

Words of Encouragement

A word aptly spoken
is like apples of gold in settings of silver.

Proverbs 25:11

An apple for the teacher is a time-honored gift. But what to give the Sunday school teacher who needs a lift? Those words "aptly spoken" are gifts that encourage and build up fellow workers for God.

Focus on reading the Scriptures to the church, encouraging the believers, and teaching them.

1 Timothy 4:13 (NLT)

"You Are Christ's Arms"

Feel the call of God in your ministry. You are the teacher sent from God. You are the model after whom children will pattern their Christian responses. As the arms of Christ, you can embrace and encourage; as the voice of Christ you can lead people to see how worthy and acceptable they are. You are the front line, receiving the "soldiers" from the front lines of school, family pressures, peers, and failure. How you respond represents the response of Christ. Is that too much or too scary? No. For if God called you, then he will enable and equip you.

Walter Shiffer

Ask God

Ask God daily to make you a wise teacher who makes learning a joy, and I know he will help you to be the best Sunday school teacher you can be.

Terry Hall
Author, How to Be the Best Sunday School Teacher You Can Be

But the Counselor, the Holy Spirit . . . will teach you all things and will remind you of everything I have said to you.

Jesus, in John 14:26

Safe Places

Sunday school is effective when kids have a safe place to explore God's Word and how it applies to their lives. Here adults who are discipling them regularly can pray for them specifically.

Margie Clark

The Lord's servants . . . must be kind to everyone. They must be able to teach effectively and be patient with difficult people. They should gently teach those who oppose the truth.

2 Timothy 2:24-25 (NLT)

On Feeling "Qualified"

If all Sunday school teachers waited until they were completely qualified to handle the job before they attempted to teach a class, the Sunday school would have gone belly-up over a century ago. When asked to teach a class, most people immediately think of a number of reasons to decline the invitation. Nobody feels qualified or good enough. We all think we don't have a strong enough faith or sufficient knowledge or the necessary skills and ability to work with people. Fortunately, perfection has never been a prerequisite for the position. Even Jesus picked some obviously imperfect folks to handle the task of establishing the early church, and they managed to get the job done by remembering that their teacher had said, "Lo, I am with you always."

Joanne Owens
Author, The Official Sunday School Teachers Handbook

Yes, You!
Let me slip in this moment one significant truth: You are still valuable. You count. Yes, you.

Charles R. Swindoll

The Only Person
Realize your importance as a teacher. You may be the only person in that individual's life that talks to him or her about the Lord and his Word.

T. O. Thomas

Belonging
Our vocation is nothing else but to belong to Christ. The work that we do is only a means to put our love for Christ into living action.

Mother Teresa

Rewards of Patience

Sunday school is valuable in a Christian's life because it is a place of participation and idea sharing. If a teacher is patient enough to include every student, the rewards will be immeasurable.

Preston Washington

Foundations of Faith

You don't have to know all the answers. Just be willing to share, discover, and investigate with kids while getting to know them. If you are patient, you can help create a foundation of faith for life.

Cindy Kenney
Chapel Ministries

Genuine Love

Sunday school teachers need godly character, honesty, integrity, faithfulness, commitment, patience, love, and above all else, the right message. The Holy Scriptures (Old and New Testaments) should be the only standard for faith and practice. Teaching in Sunday school must be a labor of love. We must show to every student, whether young or old, that we genuinely love him or her and care about his or her spiritual well-being.

Mike Harrison

The Turtle on the Fencepost

Alex Haley, the author of *Roots*, has a picture in his office, showing a turtle sitting atop a fence. The picture is there to remind him of a lesson he learned long ago: "If you see a turtle on a fencepost, you know he had some help."

The Pulitzer Prize-winning Haley says, "Any time I start thinking, *Wow, isn't this marvelous what I've done!* I look at that picture and remember how this turtle—me—got up on that post."

Craig Brian Larson

Nameless and Necessary

† Who taught Martin Luther his theology and inspired his translation of the New Testament?

† Who visited Dwight L. Moody at a shoe store and spoke to him about Christ?

† Who was the wife of Charles Haddon Spurgeon?

† Who refreshed the apostle Paul in that Roman dungeon as he wrote his last letter to Timothy?

† Who found the Dead Sea Scrolls?

† Who encouraged Catherine Marshall to write about her late husband, Peter?

† Who was Henrietta Mears's Sunday school teacher?

Most people couldn't answer even one of the above—but these unknown servants, however nameless, were also very *necessary* to the kingdom.

Charles R. Swindoll, adapted

For Eternity

A teacher affects eternity; he can never tell where his influence stops.

Henry Brooks Adams

A Prayer for His Presence

Dear Jesus, help me to spread your fragrance wherever I go. Flood my soul with your Spirit and life. Penetrate and possess my whole being so utterly that my life may only be a radiance of yours. Shine through me and be so in me that every soul I come in contact with may feel your presence in my soul.

A prayer by Cardinal John Henry Newman

Jesus and the Twelve Decibels

True Tales from the Sunday-School Front

The cheerful heart has a continual feast.

Proverbs 15:15

Christian educators may teach Truth. But sometimes things happen that seem more like fiction. . . .

Better Than Flannelgraph
I know all about it. I've got the video.

A four year old when his teacher asked
what he knew about the story of Daniel in the lions' den

Oh, By the Way . . .
In 1982–83, I taught a large high school Sunday school class. One day, in the middle of teaching, I noticed an orange glow out of the corner of my eye. I turned, and there was John, a skinny sophomore, lighting the fringe on the legs of his blue jeans and watching the cotton fibers glow and then burn out. I said, "John, do you realize that if you set your jeans on fire, you're in them?"

"Oh," he said. Apparently, he hadn't thought of that.

Kevin A. Miller

Even Billy Graham!

One day [when I was a boy] I was visiting an aunt who ordered us to spend some time reading the Bible. In about ten minutes, I went back to her and boasted, "I just read a whole book in the Bible." She thought I was a remarkable boy. (I had discovered the Epistle of Jude, the shortest book in the New Testament. One page!)

Billy Graham

Elephants, Ducks, and Geese

One summer at church, I taught the four- and five-year-olds' class, the Elephants. I was fortunate to have the pastor's son, Nate, in my class. He took me under his wing and showed me the ropes.

"I'm the oldest," he proudly told me in his best, wise five-year-old manner.

"Uh, Nate, I think I've got you beat there," I said in my best over-thirty adult manner.

He gave me a patient look like you'd give a pet who had just performed a cute trick. "I'm the oldest *kid* here," he said, all but patting me on the head.

A typical Sunday went as follows. After the Bible story and worship time, and after another of Nate's reminders that he was the oldest, there was free time. After fifty different suggestions for activities were given, usually Nate would pipe up, "Let's play Duck, Duck, Goose!" This was then promptly seconded by the other children.

I then turned to my handy curriculum guide, which did not list "Duck, Duck, Goose" as an option. Finally, I gave in and allowed them to play. Somehow Duck, Duck, Goose became a necessary addition to our class time each week!

Linda Washington

Topic A

"We're talking about Jesus again? All we ever talk about is Jesus, Jesus, Jesus!"

Mario, age 4, as said to his teacher Gia Washington

For the Bible Tells Me So

Here are a few scriptural accounts, as seen through the eyes of young "Bible scholars" from around the world. . . .

☻ God got tired of creating the world, so he took the Sabbath off. Adam and Eve were created from an apple tree. The First Commandment is when Eve told Adam to eat the apple.

☻ Moses led the Hebrews to the Red Sea, where they made unleavened bread made without any ingredients. The Egyptians were all drowned in the desert. Afterward, Moses went up on Mount Cyanide to get the Ten Commandments. Moses died before he ever reached Canada. Then Joshua led the Hebrews in the Battle of Geritol. The greatest miracle in the Bible is when Joshua told his son to stand still and he obeyed him.

☻ David was a Hebrew king skilled at playing the liar. He fought with the Finklesteins, a race of people who lived in biblical times.

☻ Jesus enunciated the Golden Rule, which says to do one to others before they do one to you. The people who followed the Lord were called the Twelve Decibels. One of the opossums was St. Matthew, who was by profession a taximan.

⊛ St. Paul cavorted to Christianity. He preached holy acrimony, which is another word for marriage. A Christian should have one wife. This is called monotony.

Edward K. Rowell

Did You Know . . .

*Surprising Sunday School
Facts and Figures*

Your word, O Lord, is eternal;
   it stands firm in the heavens.
Your faithfulness continues through all generations;
   you established the earth, and it endures.
Your laws endure to this day,
   for all things serve you.

                                      Psalm 119:89-91

Here are a few surprising facts even the most veteran Sunday school teachers may not know:

📖 Although Englishman Robert Raikes is known as the "Father of Sunday School" and is credited for its beginnings in the 1780s, a woman named Hannah Ball deserves some credit. Ball, a Methodist, had people in her home for Sunday instruction in 1763. Of course, John Wesley also taught children on Sunday in about 1735 as a missionary in Georgia. Raikes, however, did start Sunday charity schools (also known as "ragged schools") for poor children in Gloucester, England. By 1787 there were 250,000 children enrolled.

📖 By 1859, the Sunday school movement had provided three-fifths of the libraries in America.

📖 The song "Jesus Loves Me" became a popular Sunday school song due to a best-selling book called *Say and Seal* by Anna and Susan Warner, published in 1860. The sisters taught West Point cadets on Sunday. The song was set to music by William Bradbury in 1861.

📖 Dwight L. Moody's involvement in the Sunday school movement helped give it a "second birth" starting at the Illinois Sunday School Convention during the 1860s.

📖 When Lucy Maud Montgomery first began writing *Anne of Green Gables*, she thought of it as a series for a Sunday school take-home paper. After later marrying a minister, Montgomery became active in Sunday school.

📖 Over 44 million people attend Sunday school each week.

📖 Former president Jimmy Carter has taught Sunday school since he was eighteen. Other civic leaders like John D. Rockefeller and John Wanamaker also taught Sunday school.

Walk worthy of the vocation wherewith ye are called.
Ephesians 4:1 (KJV)

Sources Cited

Carter, Jimmy, *Living Faith* (New York: Times Books/Random House, 1996)

Carter, Jimmy, *Sources of Strength* (New York: Times Books, 1997)

Graham, Billy, *Just As I Am* (New York: Harper Collins, 1997)

Hall, Terry, *How to Be the Best Sunday School Teacher You Can Be* (Chicago: Moody Press, 1986)

Larson, Craig Brian, ed., *Illustrations for Preaching & Teaching: From Leadership Journal* (Grand Rapids, Mich.: Baker Book House, 1993)

LeFever, Marlene, *Creative Teaching Methods* (Colorado Springs: Cook Ministries Resources, 1985)

LeFever, Marlene, *Learning Styles: Reaching Everyone God Gave You to Teach* (Colorado Springs: Cook Ministries Resources, 1995)

Successful Sunday School (video), David C. Cook Publishing Co., 1983

Mother Teresa, *Loving Jesus* (Ann Arbor, Mich.: Servant Publications, 1991)

Mother Teresa, *Heart of Joy* (Ann Arbor, Mich.: Servant Books, 1987)

Owens, Joanne, *The Official Sunday School Teachers Handbook* (Colorado Springs: Meriwether Publishing, 1987)

Rowell, Edward K., ed., *Humor for Preaching & Teaching: From Leadership Journal & Christian Reader* (Grand Rapids, Mich.: Baker Book House, 1996)

Swindoll, Charles R., *Encourage Me* (Grand Rapids, Mich.: Zondervan, 1982)

Teacher Touch, ed. by Marlene LeFever (David C. Cook Church Ministries)

Towns, Elmer, *The Successful Sunday School and Teachers Guidebook* (Carol Stream, Ill.: Creation House, 1976)

Sources for Facts:

Bruce, Harry, *Maud: The Life of L. M. Montgomery* (New York: Seal Bantam, 1992)

Lynn, Robert W., and Elliot Wright, *The Big Little School: Two Hundred Years of The Sunday School* (New York: Harper & Row, 1971)

Linda Washington comes from a family of Sunday school teachers (and students). She is a writer based in Carol Stream, a suburb of Chicago, with extensive experience in textbook and Sunday school curriculum development.